The Hidden Secrets for
Understanding Women

Everything I want my
sons to know.

JRemingtonPress.com

© Copyright 2023 J Remington Press

All rights reserved

ISBN: 979-8-9856101-4-7

Instructions: *"Wait, hold it!"* you say, *"a journal needs no instructions? It's paper with lines. Every nincompoop knows that you pay a lot for some paper, bound into a cool looking cover so your friends think you're a smarty pants when you drag it around with you."*

So is this a journal? *Yes!* Is it a notebook. *Yes!* Is it a lecture series? *Yes!* Is it a joke book? *Yes!* But too often the joke is on us men when we blunder oblivious through life. If nothing more, use this journal to work through some of your own oblivious male issues.

Of all the poignant, humorous, insightful, and clever things we read, hear, and think we understand about women; No insights will be more important to your sons than the ones you garner from your life experiences with their mother, not to mention **your** mother, sisters, aunts, grandmothers, daughters and even the girl next door.

Take notes! Take notes that can help your sons navigate the mysterious, magical and glorious creatures we call women.

Its now up to you to share the hidden secrets you discover about the women you love, you tolerate, you honor, you fear and you cherish. Give your sons a head start.

Whether you fill every page, write a single sentence or a single word in this journal, the way you treat your son's mother teaches them far more than your chicken scratches ever will.

So what kind of book is this? ***It's the book you write!***

On the next page you'll find a quote I found extremely poignant about the magic of womanhood.

Although Abigail was addressing women, an important thing I want my sons to know and appreciate, are some of the struggles their sisters, their girlfriends, their wives and their daughters experience as they grow and mature. Thank you for indulging this use of one of your note pages.

Start paying attention, and start taking notes...

"Becoming a woman means losing a body almost indistinguishable from a boy's in terms of strength and solidity, and growing into one that is softer, more sexually inviting, but more vulnerable, too.

For the first few years, you can feel like a hermit crab who has outgrown a shell it must then abandon, blindly scurrying for another. The armor you eventually take up is of a different sort. You can no longer credibly challenge the boys to an arm-wrestling match and expect to win.

Forced to rely on subtler talents, you develop them. You learn to strike with a glance; you learn to soothe with one too. If done right, you fill your quiver with words, humor, intrigue, and emotion. You'll spend a lifetime learning when to deploy each to greatest effect—and when to forbear and offer none.

But for Pete's sake, whatever type of women young girls become, they should all listen to feminists of a prior era and stop taking sex stereotypes seriously. A young woman can be an astronaut or a nurse; a girl can play with trucks or with dolls. And she may find herself attracted to men or to other women. None of that makes her any less of a girl or any less suited to womanhood.

Young women have more educational and career options today than they ever have. Remember to tell your daughter that. Tell her also that a woman's most unique capacity—childbirth—is perhaps life's greatest blessing. But whatever else you teach your daughter, remember to include something more. Tell her because the culture so often denies it. Tell her because people will try to make a victim of her. Tell her because it's natural to doubt. Most of all, tell her because it's true. <u>She's lucky. She's special. She was born a girl. And being a woman is a gift, containing far too many joys to pass up.</u>"

    - Abigail Shrier

Understanding Women

> "The problem with life is, by the
> time you can read women like a
> book, your library card has expired."
> – Milton Berle

Everything I Want My Sons to Know

"Having kids—the responsibility of rearing good, kind, ethical, responsible human beings—is the biggest job anyone can embark on."
– Maria Shriver

Understanding Women

> "We have a secret in our culture,
> and it's not that birth is painful. It's
> that women are strong."
> – Laura Stavoe Harm

> "To understand one woman is not necessarily to understand any other woman."
> – John Stuart Mill

Understanding Women

"When a woman says, 'I have nothing to wear!', what she really means is, 'There's nothing here for who I'm supposed to be today.'"
– Caitlin Moran

Everything I Want My Sons to Know

"No man succeeds without a good woman behind him. Wife or mother, if it is both, he is twice blessed indeed."
Godfrey Winn

Understanding Women

"You should never say anything to a
woman that even remotely suggests
that you think she's pregnant
unless you can see an actual baby
emerging from her at that moment."
– Dave Barry

"There are two theories to arguing
with a woman. Neither works."
– Will Rogers

Understanding Women

> "You don't just help create a mother, you help create a mother bear. The rest of your life must be dedicated to cherish, love and support her. She needs you most when she starts to growl."
> Joseph Remington

"I don't think anyone can teach you
how to be a man but a woman.
You only learn by learning what
they need."
– Ryan Gosling

Understanding Women

> "Men and women play the same game but with different rules."
> – Habeeb Akande

Everything I Want My Sons to Know

"No matter how happily a woman may be married, it always pleases her to discover that there is a nice man who wishes that she were not."
– H.L. Mencken

Understanding Women

"A woman can say more in a sigh than a man can say in a sermon."
– Arnold Haultain

"If women didn't exist, all the money in the world would have no meaning."
– Aristotle Onassis

Understanding Women

"After about twenty years of marriage, I'm finally starting to scratch the surface of that one, (understanding women) and I think the answer lies somewhere between conversation and chocolate."
– Mel Gibson

"Men learn to love the woman they
are attracted to. Women learn to
become attracted to the man they
fall in love with."
– Woody Allen

Understanding Women

"One ounce of mother is
worth a pound of clergy."
- Rudyard Kipling

"It was one of those puzzling facts
of life that women either celebrated
a happy event or solved their
problems with a shopping spree."
- E.A. Bucchianeri

Understanding Women

"When dating a girl, don't be
naughty! One day she will serve
with your wife in the P.T.A.
– Kent Merrell

"Always open the door for a woman.
If she doesn't want you to act like a
gentleman, it's her problem."
– Joseph Remington

Understanding Women

"She openeth her mouth with wisdom; and in her tongue is the law of kindness. She looketh well to the ways of her household, and eateth not the bread of idleness."
- Proverbs 31:26-27

Everything I Want My Sons to Know

"Some women (and here I'm referring to my wife) can share as many as three days' worth of feelings about an event that took eight seconds to actually happen."
- Dave Barry

Understanding Women

"To the bachelor, the language of
women is mystery. In those matters,
a married man is already a scholar"
- Bangambiki Habyarimana

Everything I Want My Sons to Know

"What a strange thing man is; and
what a stranger thing woman."
– Lord Byron

Understanding Women

"I believe that women have a
capacity for understanding and
compassion which man
structurally does not have."
– Barbara Jordan

"Good-looking girls break hearts,
and goodhearted girls mend them."
– Mignon McLaughlin

Understanding Women

> "I believe the choice to become a mother is the choice to become one of the greatest spiritual teachers there is."
> – Oprah

Everything I Want My Sons to Know

"Beauty is the first present nature gives
to women, and the first it takes away."
– Fay Weldon

Understanding Women

"Women have a passion for mathematics. They divide their age in half, double the price of their clothes, and always add at least five years to the age of their best friend."
– Marcel Achard

Everything I Want My Sons to Know

"Don't cheat on them. It may seem foolproof, but girls tell each other everything about everything. Trust me, they WILL find out!"
– Anonymous

Understanding Women

> "A woman will NOT be grateful at all for those submissive behaviors. She'll actually treat you like dirt if you display those behaviors!"
> – Anonymous

Everything I Want My Sons to Know

"Women always worry about the things that men forget; men always worry about the things women remember."
– Anonymous

Understanding Women

"Man has will, but woman has her way."
– Oliver Wendell Holmes

"Some men spend a lifetime in an attempt to comprehend the complexities of women. Others preoccupy themselves with somewhat simpler tasks, such as understanding the theory of relativity!"
- Albert Einstein

Understanding Women

"Women have more imagination
than men. They need it to tell us
how wonderful we are."
- Arnold H. Glasow

Everything I Want My Sons to Know

"When my wife says she'll be ready in
5 minutes, I know I have just enough
time to fly to space and write a poem
on the moon before we go."
- Mike Vanatta

Understanding Women

> "All pretty girls are a trap, a pretty trap, and men expect them to be."
> – Tennessee Williams

"Feminine intuition is a fiction
and a fraud. It is nonsensical,
illogical, emotional, ridiculous, and
practically foolproof."
- Harry Haenigsen

Understanding Women

> "There are a number of mechanical devices which increase sexual arousal, particularly in women. Chief among these is the Mercedes-Benz 380SL convertible."
> – P. J. O'Rourke

"Being the protector means you haul the baby carrier, the diaper bag and let your wife enter the chapel first and choose the pew she wants."
- A. K. Merrell

Understanding Women

"Most women set out to try to change a man, and when they have changed him they do not like him."
- Marlene Dietrich

Everything I Want My Sons to Know

"Anyone who says he can see
through women is missing a lot."
- Groucho Marx

Understanding Women

"God is the best inventor ever. He took a rib from a man and created a loudspeaker."
- Anonymous

> "Being a woman is a terribly difficult task since it consists principally in dealing with men."
> – Joseph Conrad

Understanding Women

> "The most terrifying thing any woman can say to me is 'Notice anything different?'"
> - Mike Vanatta

Everything I Want My Sons to Know

"In a perfect world, all of a woman's issues could be fixed with WD-40 and duct tape."
- Jason Love

Understanding Women

> "To judge from the covers of countless women's magazines, the two topics most interesting to women are (1) Why men are all disgusting pigs, and (2) How to attract men."
> - Dave Barry

Everything I Want My Sons to Know

"Women aren't confusing. They're a Sudoku-Jenga-puzzle surrounded by Rubix cubes strapped to a terrorist screaming at you in another language."
- Mike Vanatta

Understanding Women

"My last girlfriend had a memory so
good she could remember things
that never happened."
- Greg Tamblyn

Everything I Want My Sons to Know

"Women are definitely more interested in muscles than a sense of humor. You will never hear a woman say, "I wish Brad Pitt would put his shirt back on and tell some jokes."
- Dave Barry

Understanding Women

"Who can find a virtuous woman?
For her price is far above rubies."
Proverbs 31:10

Everything I Want My Sons to Know

"Women have every reason to be
as picky as they possibly can be,
because they bear the brunt of the
catastrophe of childrearing."
- Jordan Peterson

Understanding Women

> "The creation of women was the crowning and final and most glorified moment of human creation."
> - Jeffrey R Holland

Everything I Want My Sons to Know

"Women want to know about your ex-girlfriends, but only to confirm that she is better. You better have proven that already!"
- Joseph Remington

Understanding Women

> "Your mother, does more, gives more, loves more, sacrifices more, picks up & cleans up more than you'll ever repay. Start, with a simple thank you.
> - Captain JR Bentley

Everything I Want My Sons to Know

"All great change in America begins
at the dinner table."
– Ronald Reagan

Understanding Women

"Agreeable people are compassionate and polite. And agreeable people get paid less than disagreeable people for the same job. Women are more agreeable than men."
- Jordan Peterson

"There are few things more
powerful than the faithful prayers
of a righteous mother."
— Boyd K. Packer,

Understanding Women

"When she says she is approaching forty, don't ask her from what direction."
- Bob Hope, probably.

Everything I Want My Sons to Know

"A nuclear reactor is a lot like a woman. You just have to read the manual and press the right buttons."
- Homer Simpson

Understanding Women

"In the Lord's plan, it takes two—a man and a woman—to form a whole. Indeed, a husband and wife are not two identical halves, but a wondrous, divinely determined combination of complementary capacities and characteristics."
— Richard G. Scott

"If women were in charge and there WAS a military conflict, everybody involved would feel just awful and there would soon be a high-level exchange of notes written on greeting cards with flowers on the front, followed by a Peace Luncheon (which would be salads, with the dressing on the side)."
- Dave Barry

Understanding Women

> "People wonder what we do for our women. I'll tell you what we do. We get out of their way and look with wonder at what they're accomplishing."
> - Gordon B. Hinckley

Everything I Want My Sons to Know

"My mother was the most beautiful woman I ever saw. All I am I owe to my mother."
- George Washington

Understanding Women

> "A sensible woman can never be happy with a fool."
> - President George Washington

"She loves you for who you are. If she didn't, then why would she waste her time trying to change you?"
- Anonymous

Understanding Women

"To a real woman, competence and courage are the two most attractive characteristics a man can have. Don't believe it if she says it's your money."
- Lord Remington

Everything I Want My Sons to Know

"Women bring with them into the world a certain virtue, a divine gift that makes them adept at instilling such qualities as faith, courage, empathy, and refinement in relationships and in cultures."
- D. Todd Christofferson

Understanding Women

> "She likes your mystery. Like your extensive collection of Pokémon cards. Keep it that way."
> – Grandma Lilly

"She notices when your mom
picks out the gift."
- Your Sister

Understanding Women

> "She wants you to be thoughtful. The best presents are the ones that come from the heart, like carving out time in your day to see a movie together."
> – Alexander Hincher

"She wants to look good for you.
So don't tell her that every option
looks the same."
- Rudy Fairchild

Understanding Women

"Be the man in the relationship when they need you to be, like when it's time to kill a spider."
- Anonymous

Everything I Want My Sons to Know

"You educate a man; you educate
a man. You educate a woman; you
educate a generation."
- Brigham Young

Understanding Women

> "To call woman the weaker sex is a libel; it is man's injustice to woman. If by strength is meant brute strength, then, indeed, is woman less brute than man. If by strength is meant moral power, then woman is immeasurably man's superior.
> - Mahatma Gandhi

Everything I Want My Sons to Know

"She likes it when you do gentlemen-like things. She likes it better when you genuinely are a gentleman."
Dr. Alexander Cavinaugh

Understanding Women

> "Women are very capable of solving their emotional problems themselves. Sometimes they just need someone who listens to their story without them saying what's right or wrong."
> – Every Smart Man

Everything I Want My Sons to Know

"Above all, your woman just wants
the two of you to be happy together.
This is way more simple than any list
of what a woman wants."
- Joseph Remington

Understanding Women

"Men will spend 2 dollars on a 1 dollar
item that they desperately need.
Women will spend 1 dollar on a 2 dollar
item that they don't need at all."
- Common Knowledge

Everything I Want My Sons to Know

"If you want something said, ask a man; if you want something done, ask a woman."
- Prime Minister Margaret Thatcher

Understanding Women

"I have an idea that the phrase weaker sex was coined by some woman to disarm some man she was preparing to overwhelm."
– Ogden Nasho

"I love women. They're the best thing ever created. If they want to be like men and come down to our level, that's fine."
– Mel Gibson

Understanding Women

> "I hate women because they always know where things are."
> – James Thurber

Everything I Want My Sons to Know

"High heels were invented by a woman
who had been kissed on the forehead."
– Christopher Morley

Understanding Women

"A kind heart he hath; a woman
would run through fire and water
for such a kind heart."
— William Shakespeare,
The Merry Wives of Windsor

Everything I Want My Sons to Know

"A man's face is his autobiography. A woman's face is her work of fiction."
– By Oscar Wilde

Understanding Women

> "The amount of hair they shed is unreal... Not sure how they still have a full body of hair on their head after a week."
> - Preferred Anonymity

"They don't want your advice, they don't want a calm, rational discussion about what they can do to make a situation better. Don't pour kerosene on that fire, just let it burn out."
-Wise old saying

Understanding Women

> "Do you not know I am a woman?
> When I think, I must speak."
> - William Shakespeare,
> As You Like It

Everything I Want My Sons to Know

"There is nothing on this earth as glorious as a wonderful woman. There is also nothing this earth as frightening as a wretched one."
- Male Patient, St. James Hospital, Room B-5

Understanding Women

"The world and all things in the world are precious but the most precious thing in the world is a virtuous woman."
- Muhammad

"Mostly I love my wife's ability to turn a living space into something safe, warm, and welcoming. A woman's touch is really something special."
- Kent Merrell

Understanding Women

> "Don't be fooled by her constantly forgetting where her keys and phone and stuff are, she'll definitely remember what you said word-for-word September 3, 2016 at 8:21 PM."
> – Anonymous

Everything I Want My Sons to Know

"Woman's bodies are amazing, fun, and terrifying in different times and situations."
- Husband
in Witness Protection Program

Understanding Women

"I learned that women find you attractive mostly for what you do and how you do it, rather than how you look. Guys are more visual in that sense."
- Max Lagnar

"The best property a man can have is a remembering tongue (about Allah), a grateful heart and a believing wife who helps him in his faith."
- Muhammad

Understanding Women

"Make-up is expensive."
- Hidden Identity

Everything I Want My Sons to Know

"You don't have enough hangers."
- Ancient Proverb

JRemingtonPress.com

www.ingramcontent.com/pod-product-compliance
Lightning Source LLC
Chambersburg PA
CBHW051129050526
R18244700001B/R182447PG44119CBX00001B/1